Stuff and Nonsense

This latest collection of light-hearted verse by
Gordon Bailey will be welcomed by his many fans,
and enjoyed by all.

Gordon likes to call his jottings 'stuff'. And good
stuff it is. Whether it is *all* 'nonsense' readers must
judge for themselves. The poet simply hopes to raise
a smile – and get under the reader's skin.

The pictures are the work of Gordon's illustrator
son, Andrew Bailey.

GORDON BAILEY is currently Executive Director
of Schools Outreach. His first 'piece' was published
when he was ten. He is the author of several books
of verse and compiler of the anthology *100
Contemporary Christian Poets*. His work has been
broadcast and televised.

STUFF
AND
NONSENSE

A Collection of Verse and Worse

by
GORDON BAILEY

A LION PAPERBACK
Oxford · Batavia · Sydney

Copyright © 1989 Gordon Bailey
Illustrations copyright © 1989 Andrew Bailey

Published by
Lion Publishing plc
Sandy Lane West, Littlemore, Oxford, England
ISBN 0 7459 1828 X
Albatross Books Pty Ltd
PO Box 320, Sutherland, NSW 2232, Australia
ISBN 0 7324 0145 3

First edition 1989

All rights reserved

Acknowledgment
Some of the stuff in this book appeared in previous books:

Plastic World STL Publications 1971
Mothballed Religion STL Publications 1972
Patchwork Quill SOL Publications 1975
Can A Man Change? STL Publications 1979

Much of the material, though frequently performed, has not been
published until now.

British Library Cataloguing in Publication Data
Bailey, Gordon
  Stuff and nonsense:
  a collection of verse and worse.
  I. Title
  821'.914

  ISBN 0-7459-1828-X

Printed and bound in Great Britain by
Cox and Wyman Ltd, Reading

CONTENTS

Let's Communicate!   11

I Am   12

Sunset   13

Putting Your Feet In It   14

The Ostrich   15

Albert's Last Holiday   16

Ding   19

Gone and Forgotten   20

Midwinter   21

Ding Dong   22

First Trip to Church   23

The Age of the Aquarist   27

Ding Dong Bell   28

Water   29

Er . . . um   30

The Whether Outlook   31

Little   32

Match of the Day   33

Summer   34

Chauvinist Creation   35

Little Jack   36

Something Afoot   37

Love Poem   38

The Accident   39

Little Jack Horner   42

Missus McLeod   43

The Idolater   44

5

And There Was Light   45

Time   46

The Grand Old Duke   47

Astr-illogical   48

If Only   49

Today   50

Grown-ups   51

Zzzz . . .   53

The Missing Piece   54

The Butterfly   55

Iron Horse   56

No One Tells Us How · 57

Television?   58

The Proof of the Pudding . . .   59

Tongue Twister   60

Teach Me to Cry   61

Christmas/Sacred   63

Prodigal Preoccupied   64

Freedom   66

A Frog   67

A Lack of Consideration   68

Rock-a-bye   69

Nothing New   70

Twinkle Twinkle   71

Run Rarebit Run   72

Fussy-pot   73

Mary Had . . .   74

Will the Real Jesus Please Get Lost   75
X   77
Trouble Praying?   78
Wee Willie Winkie   79
Mary Had a Little . . .   80
Good Mourning   81
The Atheist   82
Hickory, Dickory Dock   83
A Man . . .   84
Slitherside Farm   85
Babylon   89
'Where Neither Moth Nor Rust Doth Corrupt'   90
I Am a Coloured Man   91
Stretching One's Resources   92
My Telephone   93
Anarchy   94
Sol   95

STUFF AND NONSENSE?

I have always preferred to call my jottings *stuff* rather than describe them any other way. Some of my *stuff* could be considered to be *good stuff*, which seeks to say something, other of my *stuff* is nonsense.

Why write nonsense?
I have noted that even my most nonsensical stuff can bring a smile to some faces and it is my hope that my stuff and my nonsense will, at least, cause some amusement. Should some of it also cause some consideration or, even, a tendency towards radical change — that would be good.

GORDON BAILEY

LET'S COMMUNICATE!

If you wish to communicate,
On this one thing please meditate:
Avoid pretence, be real, be true,
That I might know who's really you.
Show me yourself in honesty,
And not the *you* you'd have me see.
We will not progress very far,
Unless you show me who you are.

   Yet all is lost if you don't see
   The person who is really me!

I AM

I'm sorry that I feel I must express this point of view:
Society's professed concern is sham!
For I'm judged quite completely on the basis of 'IQ',
Instead of on the basis of 'I AM'.

SUNSET

Clouds made soft by black swan's feathers
give the blood-red orb its pillow;
gentle evening zephyr gathers
wisps of blue and grey and yellow:
waves the poplars for his brushes,
washes dusk with variegation,
wafts the clouds to cool their blushes,
hallows sun with coronation,
splashes gold in every quarter,
silhouettes the night owl's flying,
ripples crimson on the water.
Who would think the day is dying?

PUTTING YOUR FEET IN IT

To stand upon your own two feet
May land you on your face;
For standing on your dignity
Is stepping into space.

*t*HE OSTRICH

A clockwork nervous breakdown
With his treasures 'neath his wings;
A non-stop, jacked-up twitching mass
Of scaffolding and strings;

The ostrich is a nervous bird,
All wild-eyed, edgy, manic;
The slightest sound of all around
Will put him in a panic;
Then, hunched the shoulders,
Twist the neck, and jerks of quick inspections,
Before, and all at once, it seems,
He runs in all directions.

ALBERT'S LAST HOLIDAY

There's a seaside town known as Cesspool,
That's noted for foul air and smog;
Where Mister and Missus Ramsbottom
Took Albert their Pekinese dog.
It was Whitsun, and Missus Ramsbottom
Had taken time off from the pit;
They'd come to the coast to relax on the beach,
But found they had nowhere to sit.
There were beer cans, and bottles, and white plastic cups,
All scattered all over the shore;
Ramsbottom complained, and he asked why they'd come,
So she said, 'It weren't like this before.'

She pointed to Albert, who'd gone for a swim,
And said, 'Why not go for a dip?'
He said, 'I'd be better to paddle in t' drains,
Or scramble about on a tip.'
Just then from a rockpool they heard Albert yelp,
Said husband, 'Now what's going on?'
So Missus Ramsbottom went over to see,
But she found that poor Albert was gone.
She peered in the water and then staggered back
With a queer sort of look in her eyes;
For there in the rockpool, near big as a bath,
Was a crab! Ee, it was a surprise.

Her husband came over and said, 'Where's the dog?'
Said she, 'There's the mark of his paws –
In the sludge by the pool, he's been swallowed by that,
See, it's got his right ear in its claws.'
Her husband peered in, then he nodded and said,
'It's that nuclear waste from the Lab.
'It's mutation that's done it.' She said, 'Don't be daft.
It were done by that ruddy great crab.'

Said he, 'I'll go in after Albert.'
Said she, 'Better take off your socks!
There's mussels as big as torpedoes —
No! Not on the crab, on the rocks.'
But Mister Ramsbottom, as brave as could be,
Not showing a morsel of fear,
Walked into the pool, made a grab and leapt out,
Saying, 'All I could get was this ear.'
The Ramsbottoms tried to save Albert in vain,
They tried every day for a week;
Said Mister to Missus, 'We'd better give up,
We just are not reaching our Peke.
We'd better complain to the council,' said he;
'I'll send them this ear with that there.'
And reaching in t' rockpool he heaved out a shrimp,
Which he sent with the ear to the mayor.

'They'll have to do summat,' he said to his wife,
'To deal with that crabby great beast.
I've mailed them first class, so they'll get them no doubt
By the end of next week at the least.'
They waited and waited but nothing occurred,
So they wrote to the local MP;
He replied sympathizing, inviting them both
To visit the Commons for tea.
He told them his party was doing its best
To tackle pollution at t' source:
They'd dogs on patrol sniffing beaches and dunes,
Avoiding the rockpools of course.
He promised them action, and promised it soon,
He promised them some recompense.
Said they, 'He's won Crufts, and he's worth quite a bit,
So we'll take it in fivers and tens.'

But all that they got for the loss of their dog,
In spite of appeals to the Lords,
Was a photo of Albert being swallowed by t' crab
In a tableau at Madame Tussauds!

ING

Ding Dong bell,
Puss is in the well;
We've put some disinfectant down
To camouflage the smell.

GONE AND FORGOTTEN

Cardmas.
Crackermas.
Tinselmas.
Jinglemas.
Turkeymas.
Puddingmas.
Stockingmas.
Drunkenmas.
Excitementmas.
Overdraftmas.
Disappointmentmas.
Alkaseltzermas!

God came down at CHRISTmas
and found it wasn't.

Nights stay longer, days are shorter,
warm-wrapped skaters walk on water;
statuesque the swans have chosen
sheltered pools as yet unfrozen.

Stark against the snow the teazel's
darker than the winter weasels.
Skies are clear, the wind is bitter,
icing branches with its glitter.

Oak is naked, holly blushes;
moorhens tiptoe through the rushes.
Tips of snowdrops now ascending,
heralding the winter's ending.

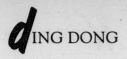ING DONG

Ding Dong bell,
Grandad's slippers smell!
That is why the rhyme has pussy
Living down the well.

fIRST TRIP TO CHURCH

The first time that I went to church
was on a Sunday mornin';
from what I'd heard I'd likely find
I'd spend the 'ole time yawnin'.
At eighteen years of age or so
I thought I knew it all;
my 'air was long, my jeans were tight,
I loved a knife or bottle fight,
providin' mates stood left and right,
and those we fought were small.

My mates and me we'd never been,
so off to church we filed;
we walked inside 'bout three abreast,
straight down the middle aisle;
some of us were smokin' fags,
others suckin' sherbets;
we sat in what they called a pew,
then looked around to see just who
would come to church — let me tell you,
they looked a load of herberts.

The row behind was full of dames,
you should've seen their looks,
then one old dear gave me a smile
and offered me some books.
I passed 'em round, we opened 'em,
you should've seen the words:
all set out like poetry is,
the words fair put us in a tizz,
and Fred said, through his lemon fizz,
'These books are for the birds.'

'Be quiet!' said someone. 'Tut, tut, tut!'
With tuts the place did buzz.
So Sam stood up and shouted,
'Grief! You make more noise than us.'
We looked around the buildin' then,
it really was revealin':
Sam said, 'Look mates, get the score?
There ain't no carpets on the floor.
See the rafters! They're so poor
they can't afford a ceilin'.'

'Can't afford electric either,
using candles everywhere;
coloured windows like me granny's,
at the bottom of her stairs.'
'Shut your face,' I said to Sammy,
'I'm for listenin', so is Ron.'
From the left, with scarce a noise,
came a line of little boys.
Sam said, in his loudest voice,
'Cor! They've all got nighties on!

'Blokes as well, with cloaks and banners,
look at that one! Must be queer!
Then they dare condemn us young 'uns
for the way we choose our gear.'
Round the church we watched 'em movin',
like a circus out on hire.
Sam said, 'Can't make out what this is,
Holy smoke!' And then he hisses,
'Where's the holy water missus?
Vicar's handbag's caught on fire.'

If looks could kill we'd all've suffered,
but they can't I'm glad to say;
then, without a lot of bother,
everythin' got under way:
first we all knelt down together,
Sammy took his trilby off,
then the vicar put his hand up,
seemed he wanted us to stand up,
'When they goin' to strike the band up?'
Sammy said, behind a cough.

It doesn't make much sense to me,
what goes in them there places;
I'd understand a little bit
if they had happy faces.
They sing of peace and happiness,
and how the joybells ring,
yet most of 'em look bored to bits,
I say, 'You load of hypocrites,
why don't you honestly admit
you don't mean what you sing?'

Then there's him what gives the preach,
the vicar, what's his name?
The hymns, the prayers, and what he says,
they're all about the same.
We went to church, we listened hard,
but what about his chat?
He talked of 'sinking, shifting sand',
used words like 'wrath' and 'reprimand'.
My mates and me don't understand
a language quite like that.

I'm used to chattin' to my mates
with words what have a meanin',
but that there church is just about
the oddest place I've been in.
If people want that nonsense, well,
then let 'em, that's okay;
but let me tell you what *I* feel:
you needs a bloke who'll learn a deal
of what it takes to make it real,
what Jesus had to say.

It seems like most religious folk
don't care that we're in need;
they hand us bits of paper
in a language we can't read.
They sit inside their churches
with nothin' in their hearts;
some try to help, but bring despair,
'cause they have nothing *real* to share,
I think those folks'll still be there
when Armageddon starts.

I only went to church to see
if they could offer hope,
but everythin' what happened there
was way outside my scope.
A workin' lad in search of truth,
they looked and let me pass;
I pleaded for a little cheer,
they all pretended not to hear,
I got the message, loud and clear,
that church was middle class.

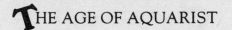THE AGE OF AQUARIST

My mind's a small aquarium, where swims a school of
    thought;
A shoal of ever-new ideals, the slowly-moving sort.
They feed on meditation, 'neath an artificial light,
Sustained within their little world, all snug and
    watertight.

The water's warmed by faith and hope, and gullibility;
While daydream-driven filters help remove reality.
A plastic-coated cover makes quite sure they stay inside:
For the last ideal to leave my mind just flapped around —
    and died!

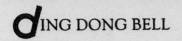DING DONG BELL

Ding Dong bell,
Pussy isn't well;
It said P-O-I-S-O-N
But pussy couldn't spell.

WATER

Springs from earth a gentle trickle,
gathers volume downward pouring;
runs beneath the green furze prickle,
from the gorge emerges roaring;
down the mountain leaps uncaring,
sprays the spectrum while cascading;
wanders lowly, wild and daring,
flowing calm 'neath willows' shading.

Swift the shallows, deeps are stiller,
here the otter and the eel
swim together. For the miller
water wheels his waterwheel.

See the twisting mist of midges
where the stream breaks rapidly
white below the moss-green bridges,
onward widening to the sea.

ЄR . . . UM

One of the greatest hindrances
To progress is
Uncertainty.
Er . . .
I think.

*t*HE WHETHER OUTLOOK

Whether I'm helpful when people despair;
Depends very largely on whether I care.
Whether I think that oppression's a crime,
Depends very largely on whether I've time.
Whether I go where my help is required,
Depends very largely on whether I'm tired.
Whether I'm generous, whether I'm mean,
Depends very largely on whether I'm keen;
Whether I honour the vows that I take,
Depends very largely on what I can make.
Whether I help someone burdened by care,
Depends very largely on whether I'm there.
Whether I love, or I hope, or I trust,
Depends very largely on whether I must.
Whether I comfort a friend who's afraid,
Depends very largely on whether I'm paid.

Whether I'll be just the same come next year,
Depends quite completely on whether I'm here!

ITTLE

Little Jack Horner
Sat in a corner
Eating his Christmas pie,
He stuck in his thumb,
Pulled out a J.C.B. Earthmover
And said,
'I could have choked on that!'

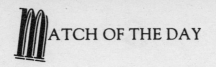ATCH OF THE DAY

Mankind is but a football in a game that's played by fools,
With no effective referee to emphasize the rules.
Yet nailed upon a crossbar is a man, born for the role,
Whom stupid men have put to death, refusing his control.
So as a consequence one finds an anarchistic game,
Where death's a commonplace affair, and no one takes
   the blame.

Within the sunlit stadium, mankind gets kicked around;
Their hopes and dreams, and high ideals, lie lifeless on
   the ground.
One commentator claims there isn't very long to play,
That most of those involved will be sent off on Final Day.
A starry universe spectates, and wonders at a sport,
Where men must fill their pens with blood, to write the
   match report!

SUMMER

God painted the clouds
and the white daisy plains
then shook out his paintbrush
all over the lanes;
the cow parsley leads me
from village to town
through byways besmattered
and scattered with down;
so I roll down my socks
and I go for a ramble,
and I damage my legs
on the gorse and the bramble.

With grass down my back
and grass in my buckle
I lie and I savour
the sweet honeysuckle;
I lie and I dream
and I dream of my lover,
we walk hand in hand
where the dragonflies hover;
I hear in the distance
a woodpecker drummer
and I'm glad for the sound
as I'm glad for the Summer.

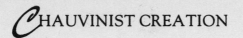CHAUVINIST CREATION

Dear Earth,
        Here is man.
                Love,
                        God.

P.S. Here is woman.

LITTLE JACK

Little Jack Horner
Sat in a corner
Eating his Christmas pie,
He stuck in his thumb,
Pulled out the Aztec Civilization
And said,
'So, that's where it went!'

SOMETHING AFOOT

I went to the doctor's, to see him of course,
I saw him, because he was in;
I'd stood on a nail which was rusty and long
and my shoe had been really worn thin.

I showed him the wound on the base of my foot,
I rambled a bit, being bad;
He asked me how was I, said, 'Get to the point.'
I told him I already had.

He ummed and he arred, then said, 'Here's what to do:
just stop everyone that you meet:
you tell them you're sorry, admitting you're sore,
you tell them you're pained by defeat.

Say "Sorry", apologize time after time,
do this and your foot will be whole.'
'How's that going to help me?' I asked. He replied:
'Confession is good for the sole!'

I leapt to my foot and I called him a twit,
I swore at him — in the nurse came.
'Now what are you doing?' she asked, so I said:
'I'm giving the doc a bad name.'

'Now tell him you're sorry,' she said, so I did,
and what this confession revealed
was that he had been right, for I took off my sock
and saw that my sole had been healed.

LOVE POEM

I held her tight,
That special night.
We kissed — a real humdinger!

I ran my hand
Through her mass of hair
And a squirrel bit my finger.

tHE ACCIDENT

We were driving in the dark
(Autumnal, cold, Friday-evening darkness),
fields sliding alongside us unseen
in utter rural blackness,
when we saw houses:
quiet and still they were,
and their unseeing eyes
(coloured blue, or green, or patterned with roses, or
    veiled with lace)
reflected on our lights;
their minds were reflecting upon images of Tom and Jerry,
or The Muppets,
or arguments about pocket money,
or loneliness;
but,
suddenly —
a brief, ugly noise.
A small family car,
containing two women,
had hit a large lorry
head on.

The houses hadn't seen it,
the accident.

Inside the houses people spoke:
'What was that?'
'An explosion?'
'Turn the telly down!'
'Quiet!'

We saw a boy running,
but we couldn't hear him.
The cars in front braked.
We stopped.
I opened the door.
I stood.
I could see,
forty yards ahead of us,
the accident.

The houses awoke,
one by one,
but not all together.
People spilled on to the roadside.
Some ran,
some stood,
a young man ran past us.

I walked towards the accident but I stopped,
knowing, I think,
that there was nothing I could do.
Was it instinct?
Was it fear?
And
what had rendered everyone silent?
There were no shouts,
no screams,
no talking,
no comment.

Three drivers assumed the road would be blocked and
    turned back
the way we had come.
The man with the torch signalled us to drive past
the accident,
to continue our journey.

We drove slowly over the shattered windscreens.
The small family saloon was
unrecognizable,
concertina-ed,
quiet.
A beige coat shrouded the dead driver of the car.
It was so very quiet.
My wife didn't look.
Our two young daughters quenched their curiosity,
with what?
Twisted metal,
windscreen wipers wiping the space where the
    windscreen had been,
and we thought of the family
which didn't yet know,
and we asked God to help them.

We left the accident behind,
but
our eyes had seen,
and our minds had made notes,
and my wife didn't sleep properly for more than a week.

And
we remember
the silence.

LITTLE JACK HORNER

Little Jack Horner
Sat in his corner
Watching the people die.
They pleaded for aid,
He knelt down and prayed,
Thinking
'Oh, what a good boy am I!'

MISSUS McCLEOD

Missus McCleod was slumbering deep,
A woman who loved her beauty sleep;
Whilst Mister McCleod was up with the lark,
Whistling, singing, bright as a spark.
He placed her breakfast on the bed,
Then wakened her. She grimly said,
'I like the food on the silver tray,
But not, my dear, at the break of day!'
She leapt from her bed as fast as a bullet
And rammed the salver down his gullet;
Then said, with glee, 'Now you've done your dining,
You're my McCleod with a silver lining!'

THE IDOLATER

'I love you,' he said, as he hugged her,
'I love you,' he said between sighs;
But she knew he adored his own image
As he looked at himself in her eyes.

AND THERE WAS LIGHT

It was as if all light and truth had fled
and I, abandoned to an inner dark despair,
feared silent death might soon approach my bed
to find me powerless there;

when, from the carol singers' lantern, gleamed
a light, made soft and gentle by the window-frost,
and hymns proclaimed new hope until, it seemed,
I knew all was not lost.

So now:
though shadows stand by me,
and death some day must be,
and knowledge comes reluctantly,
I shall not scorn the truth
that light has dawned,
nor will I doubt the life
which has been born
at Christmas.

IME

I'd love to relax with a vodka and lime,
My problem's a problem: I haven't the time!
I long to achieve while I'm still in my prime,
But I can't even fail, for I haven't the time!

My family's asking, 'Where is he? Where is he?'
I'm not where I'm needed because I'm too busy.

No time for a hobby, no time for real rest;
No time for a Sabbath, no time for what's best;
No time for my children, no time for my wife;
No time for deep friendship, no time of my life!

My phone is engaged and my mother is crying;
My diary's fulfilled and I'm thrilled to be . . . dying?

I need time when writing for finding the rhyme.
But verse becomes worse 'cause I haven't the time.
There ought to be moments no — 'hours' sublime.
There are! But I miss them — I haven't the time.

I *do* have the time, but by choices I lose it,
I *do* have the time, but I choose to abuse it!
I should use my time for the birds and the grasses,
Yet I've failed to see that *once only* time passes!

THE GRAND OLD DUKE

The Grand Old Duke of York,
he had ten thousand pounds;
he spent it all on lions
which now roam around his grounds!

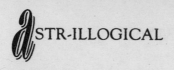STR-ILLOGICAL

We'd love to do astronomy
but we can't see the stars:
there's dirt on dad's binoculars
and clouds of dust on Mars;
Capricorn has Cancer,
that's a Sirius condition,
and Venus, though she's armless,
is not within our vision;
Leo roars inaudibly,
and we cannot seem to find
a Pole to rouse the Dog Star
or to hide the Bear behind;
Neptune's 'neath the Sea of Crises,
toastfork in his hand,
while Pluto's lost his Puppis
in the depths of Disneyland.

So we'll Plough on regardless,
seeing what the future brings,
we'll keep Orion Mercury,
and hope that Saturn rings.

We'd love to do astronomy
but dad's driven us to tears:
when we ask to watch 'The Sky at Night'
eclipse us round the ears.

IF ONLY

If only he'd faced up to living for real,
Instead of inventing the lie;
If only he hadn't believed his own dreams;
If only he'd learned how to cry.
If only he'd seen where his folly might lead,
If only he'd lifted the lid.
But he closed his mind to the truth he might find;
If only he'd not—but he did.

If only she'd questioned his motives, his aims,
If she'd only looked past his smile;
If only she'd dwelt on that glimmer of doubt,
If only she'd thought for a while.
If only she hadn't suppressed commonsense
When the eager young man made his bid;
She wouldn't be racked with regret and despair;
If only she'd not—but she did.

If only I hadn't have tried to assess
What I might achieve in return;
If only I'd offered my help to them both,
If only I'd shown some concern.
If only I'd not closed my eyes to their needs,
If I hadn't scampered and hid,
When I could have been of some use to my friends;
If only I'd not—but I did.

TODAY

Today I was introduced to a man
With a wooden leg, called George.
They didn't tell me the name of his good leg.

gROWN-UPS

They taught me to trust in the words that they said;
They taught me to walk, they taught me to talk;
They taught me to pray when I went up to bed;
They taught me a lot — grown-ups.

They taught me to scrub both my neck and my paws;
They taught me to wink, they taught me to drink;
They taught me, at Christmas, about Santa Claus;
They taught me some rot — grown-ups.

They taught me to shop; they taught me to share;
They taught me to spend, they taught me to lend;
They taught me to cuddle a large teddy bear;
They sent me to pot — grown-ups.

Now some of the things which they taught me were true,
I learned quite a bit, I'll quickly admit;
But fairies, and witches, and Winnie-the-Pooh?
What sense had they got? Grown-ups!

I started to wonder, the older I grew,
The more I would yearn to live and to learn
The things all around which were worthwhile and true;
But still I had got — grown-ups.

They started to nag when I started to smoke;
When I made them wait by stopping out late;
They yelled when I first took some rum with my coke;
They called me a clot — those grown-ups.

They started to preach and they said they knew best;
They told me of heaven when I was just seven;
I'd thrown that guff out while rejecting the rest;
I hadn't forgot — grown-ups.

I'd swallowed their lies — hook, line, sinker and rod,
But now that I knew that the most wasn't true
What reason had I to believe in their God?
Is he part of the plot, grown-ups?

They'd taught me some good, but they'd taught me some
    lies;
I'm now scared to trust, it might turn to dust,
And blow back around me and get in my eyes;
Then what have I got, grown-ups?

Just tell me how I was supposed to decide
Which stories were true? I hadn't a clue!
'Be good or the goblins will get you,' they cried;
I'm glad I'm now shot of — grown-ups.

Pretending that pixies had danced in the rain!
'Be careful,' they'd say, 'God's watching today!'
If pixies aren't real, nor is God, that is plain,
So I've dumped the lot — grown-ups.

I asked a friend if he
Attended church on Sunday mornings
Or slept late.
He said,
'Both!'

THE MISSING PIECE

He worked the jigsaw on the table-top,
engaged, involved, he simply could not stop;
his aim: to finish ere the day was done
and so he fit the many pieces one by one.
Determined that he would not know defeat
he shelved all else to make the scene complete:
a wooded hill, a river in its course,
a stone-built bridge, a girl upon a horse.

He'd almost done, each piece was in its place,
one piece to find and fit, the rider's face;
but where was it? It wasn't by his chair,
nor in the box; it wasn't anywhere.
Frustrated, tired, his temper found release:
where was that blessed missing piece?
The trees and hills were there, the sun still shone,
but the pleasure they had given him was gone.
His aim was not achieved, he'd spent a wasted day;
he broke the puzzle down and threw it all away.

Cleaning his room he was, a fortnight later,
he found the missing piece behind the radiator.
The jigsaw gone, discovery was flat . . .
How sad that some find life and God like that.
A single missing piece can so obsess:
capacity for joy becomes distress!

*t*HE BUTTERFLY

It flutters silently by:
darting
      swooping
            gently, gently,

dancing
      gliding
            softly, softly,

colourful
      elegant
            gracefully, gracefully,

welcoming the Summer,
beautifying the gardens,
attracting the eye,
edifying the mind,
uplifting the spirit,

and all because a caterpillar died!

55

IRON HORSE 1

Made by man from man's invention:
power and grace and great devotion.
Touch the trembling, taste the tension,
fused in fiery locomotion;
driving westward, furnace gleaming,
wilderness could not deter it,
ever forward, strong and steaming,
steed of pioneering spirit.

NO ONE TELLS US HOW

I hail the new philosophy
which teaches brotherhood;
which tells us how things ought to be,
encouraging the good.
We're told to aim for harmony,
to get together now;
the only fault, it seems to me,
is no one tells us how.

I welcome it when I'm advised
to search for love and peace;
perhaps I'd never realized
the need for things like these.
I'm told to find a way to free
mankind from need and care;
I'm told to search, but here's my plea:
will someone tell me where?

How can I love my enemies?
And where can I find love?
How can I know where freedom is?
And can I find enough?
If someone knows, if someone cares,
I'd like to know right now
the answer to the question, 'Where?'
The answer to the, 'How?'

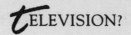ELEVISION?

BBC 1
Ask Mary Whitehouse —
'Nothing but a boob tube!'

BBC 2
Ask the young —
'For squares, a cube tube.'

ITV
Ask the advertiser —
'Go sucka Zube!' tube.

tHE PROOF OF THE PUDDING . . .

Some catering staff and some chefs booked a cruise
with a travel firm known to us all,
but something went wrong, thirteen days from Hong
    Kong,
when the ship ran aground in a squall.

The crew was all drowned when the ship ran aground,
but the chefs they all made it to shore.
A cannibal chief saw them land, said 'Good grief!
That's breakfast, lunch, dinner, and more!'

But into one pot he crammed all the lot
and then struck a match with a grin.
(Which is unusual, most people use the side of a
    matchbox.)
Said one chef, 'No complaining, at least it's not raining,
and the tour *was* described as "All-in".'

The chief watched them boiling, then yelled, 'Here,
    they're spoiling,
they're covered in fungus and froth.'
He poured them all out and said, 'There is no doubt
that too many cooks spoil the broth.'

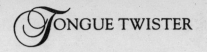

TONGUE TWISTER

I bought a pair of shoes today
But I shall have to return them —
The tongue keeps twisting
And this makes me walk with a lisp.

tEACH ME TO CRY

I witnessed an accident early today,
A young motor-cyclist had died.
I stood in the crowd, and watched for an hour;
The strange thing was — I never cried!
I thought of the driver, who sat on the kerb,
He'd blood on his neck and his chest;
I thought of the parents, who still didn't know,
But I didn't weep like the rest.
I saw a policeman with tears in his eyes,
He pulled out a large handkerchief.
I heard women sobbing, I saw a man faint,
But I never felt any grief.
I don't think that I am especially hard;
But how could I see someone die
Without feeling sorrow? For now I feel shame;
Can somebody teach me to cry?

It's not that I have no emotions at all,
I often feel angry or mad.
When things go my way, then I really feel great;
How come then I never feel sad?
I've hit out in temper; I've laughed with the boys;
I've thrilled to my girl-friend's caress;
I get quite involved with a film, or a play;
I'm sure I'm not hard to impress.
But then when it comes to a need for concern,
I find it's compassion I lack.
I tend, when I'm faced with a person in need,
To offer a view of my back.
I'm worrying now, and I'm pleading for help;
I don't think I'm such a bad guy.
I'm left out when others get worried, or fret;
Can nobody teach me to cry?

I don't want to blubber all over the place;
I don't want to howl like a kid;
I don't want to wail at a wedding or wake;
I don't want to squelch like a squid.
I just want to feel some compassion, some care;
I want to feel sorrow, to sigh;
When someone is suffering, or someone's been hurt,
I want to be able to cry.
I want to be able to help those in need;
I want to be able to earn
The right to be kind, with no motive but love;
I've come to the point where I'll learn.
So where do I go, for some teaching in love?
I need an unfailing supply!
Love breeds understanding, and patience, and trust;

Please, God, will you teach me to cry?

CHRISTMAS/SACRED
or
CHRIST/MASSACRED

Where do I draw the line?

PRODIGAL PREOCCUPIED

Disillusioned, discouraged, dejected; his resources
   dissipated;
The Prodigal determined to seek reconciliation
With Father and Home.
But on his journey
He was waylaid by a septet of female strangers:

Miss Apprehend, a pseudo-scientist,
Offered him an unproven theory
That his father didn't exist.

Miss Givings, an agnostic,
Said to him that if there was such a person as 'father',
And a place called 'home',
She didn't know about them.

Miss Belief, calling herself an atheist,
Bluntly said that there was no such place as 'home',
And no such person as 'father'.

Miss Taken, a pseudo-psychoanalyst,
Suggested that he had a father-fixation,
And that 'home' was but a dream fantasy.
She also suggested treatment at 25 guineas a session.

Miss Informed, a cynic,
Smiled at him, with curled lip,
And mocked his every step.

Miss Guided, a humanist,
Told him he didn't need a father,
And that the fulfilment of his needs
Could be found only within himself.

Miss Chief, a liberal theologian,
Told him, glibly, that his father was dead!

The father, a very real father,
A very out-of-breath father,
Running to meet the Prodigal,
Stopped
Then wept tears of love
As he saw the fast-disappearing
Figure of his son, with back turned,
Moving even further away.

The Prodigal meanwhile, armed with an aerosol spray,
Marched back towards the pigsty,
Determined to make the best
Of the very worst.

REEDOM

Personal liberty is doing as I please.
Political liberty is voting for whom I please.
Physical liberty is eating what I please,
Exercizing when I please (or not at all),
Making love to whom I please,
Going where I please.
Intellectual liberty is thinking as I please,
Reading what I please,
Hearing what I please,
Seeing what I please,
Saying what I please,
Emotional liberty is feeling how I please,
Reacting how I please.

Spiritual liberty is Freedom!

FROG

A frog he would a-wooing go!

But,
not being an owl,
he could only go
croak, croak!

a LACK OF CONSIDERATION

Just fancy being born at Christmas!
(The time of those five go-old rings.)
There's plenty to think of at Christmas
so why go and complicate things?
He could have been born during August,
or in March, or even September;
with greetings, and parties, and presents,
I've already lots to remember.
Then:
I'm eating, or watching the telly,
or hanging the glittery trim,
or doing the last-minute shopping,
and they start going on about . . . Him.
You'd have thought he'd consider the timing
of the date that he chose to appear;
you'd have thought he'd have known about Christmas . . .
it's our busiest time of the year!

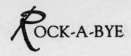OCK-A-BYE

Rock-a-bye baby outside the pub,
Your dad's getting drunk
in the Working Man's Club;
I've had a rough day,
and I've worked up a thirst;
you're wanting your bottle?
I'm wanting mine first.

Rock-a-bye baby please don't you cry,
Your dad's not to blame
and neither am I.
You'll find when you're older,
when money's all spent,
That grown-ups never take the blame,
they blame the government.

NOTHING NEW

I was told that there was nothing new
Under the sun.
So,
I looked above the sun!

tWINKLE TWINKLE

Twinkle twinkle little star,
How we wonder what you are.
Man, with his astronomy,
Seeks to probe your mystery.
Distant, timeless, infinite,
Thought-provoking little light;
Are you there by God's intent,
Or by astral accident?
One thing's certain little star,
Twinkle twinkle there you are!

RUN RAREBIT RUN

Run Rarebit run
The cheese is underdone.

FUSSY-POT

Fussy-pot, fussy-pot, where have you been?
'To London I went to condemn the obscene!'
Fussy-pot, fussy-pot, what did you there?
'I carried a sandwich board round Leicester Square!
My trousers they burst, for I wore them too tight.
How strange that my sign read "The End is in Sight!"'

Mary Had...

Mary had a little lamb,
The soft and cuddly kind,
Its only fault was obvious:
It had a huge behind.
It sat upon a gentleman
Who'd had a drop of ale;
His dying words are famous now:
'And thereby hangs a tail.'

WILL THE REAL JESUS PLEASE GET LOST

I like to think of Jesus as a decent sort of chap,
you know the sort of character I mean:
he's neither God in human form, nor is he just a myth,
but someone sort of somewhere in between.
He's meek and mild, a good example, talks a lot of sense,
a help when other help cannot be found;
a universal balsam who can soothe a troubled soul;
a handy sort of bloke to have around.
I picture him as someone who completely understands:
he sees my sins but smiles and lets them pass.
He's handsome and clean-shaven, he's broadminded and
    polite;
he's Protestant, and upper Middle Class.
He doesn't raise the dead (I'd find that way beyond belief),
he doesn't carry nail-scars in his hands;
respectable, acceptable, a friend who'll give his all,
yet never come to me and make demands.

A Superstar philosopher who's gentle and serene,
a Jesus who is popular and kind;
a Jesus who is not dogmatic, not intolerant;
a Jesus with an ever open mind.
I want my Jesus happy, bringing peace and brotherhood;
the subject of an all-embracing creed;
a theme for songs and poetry; a reasonable man,
approving of the life I choose to lead.
I like to think of him as one not difficult to please,
who'll tolerate that self-indulgent vice,
providing that I help my needy neighbour now and then,
and go to church each season once or twice.
For, after all, I celebrate his birthday every year,
with pudding, and perhaps a turkey leg;
I bring to mind his crucifixion with a hot cross bun,
recall his resurrection with an egg.

I've been accused of making up a Christ to suit myself,
who doesn't match the Christ of history.
I'm told I've compromised the truth, but let me make it
  clear:
the Jesus of the Bible's not for me.
The Jesus of the Gospels asked too much from gentle folk,
he said some things I think are very odd;
he set the standard far too high, demanding holiness,
and said he was the only way to God.
He slammed sincere religious folk, he said that they were
  wrong,
that they must follow him and him alone.
I can't accept a Christ who will not water down his
  claims,
I'm sticking with the Jesus who's my own.

A Jesus who is sinless, who's infallibly divine,
who tells me I must share his Calvary,
is not the one I'd choose, because in no respect at all
does that sort of Jesus Christ resemble me!

#

X is a kiss;
X means multiplication;
X denotes my political choice;
X is an illiterate man's name;
X means I got the sum wrong;
X is a request for anonymity;
Xmas!

TROUBLE PRAYING?

You said you find it hard to pray,
Your prayer times empty pass;
The air it feels like granite
And the ceiling seems like brass!

You said your prayers don't go beyond
The room, that you feel static.
The ceiling? Who has told you that
God lives inside your attic?

Whoever told you had it wrong,
Misplacing God's true venue:
The truth is, once invited there,
That God resides within you.

WEE WILLIE WINKIE

Wee Willie Winkie climbs up the stairs;
Wee Willie Winkie kneels to say his prayers:
Hands together, eyes closed, a bowing of his head
Mumbles words his mother taught him—tumbles into bed.

Wee Willie Winkie never fails to pray;
Wee Willie Winkie knows just what to say.
Wee Willie wonders what good the words have done,
For never has he prayed a prayer with words that are his
  own.

MARY HAD A LITTLE . . .

Mary had a little lamb,
She taught it the guitar;
It now plays in a bleat group
At the local Coffee Baaaa!

*g*OOD MOURNING

I attended an odd
but happy funeral today:
good grief!

There were four
drunken bishops present:
good grashes!

There was one
High Court judge:
good Lord!

The vicar was a Welshman:
good Evans!

The dead man was
Sir John Twinkle, philanthropist:
good knight!

The funeral, I was told,
was a bargain at the price:
good buy!

THE ATHEIST

He looked at me
straight in the eye,
polished his spectacles,
and, without even the hint of a smile,
said,
'I am an atheist,
thank God!'

HICKORY, DICKORY DOCK

Hickory, dickory dock, the preacher watched the clock;
The clock struck one, he carried on!
Hickory, dickory dock.

Hickory, dickory dock, the preacher forgot the clock;
The clock struck two, he wasn't through!
Hickory, dickory dock.

Hickory, dickory dock, the people watched the clock;
The clock struck three, he still felt 'free'!
Hickory, dickory dock.

Hickory, dickory dock, a deacon watched the clock;
The clock struck four, they still had more!
Hickory, dickory dock.

Hickory, dickory dock, the deacon stopped the clock!
But he couldn't stop the preacher!

a MAN . . .

A man knocked on our door last night
with a beard;
We didn't hear him.

SLITHERSLIDE FARM

So they came face to face:
pointing his guitar at his old man
and twanging a discord.
Pete said, staccato-like,
'Gimme what's mine!
You've been scratching round
this chicken farm for fifty years,
with no returns,
no fun,
no nothing.
This god-forsaken hole makes me sick,
I'll have what's coming to me,
I quit!
It's me for the Wicked City.'

So Pete's dad coughed up,
with no complaints.
Pete waved tattybye to his big brother
(the sucker — always working),
and sauntered away
ten thousand quid the richer.

He called at the first club he found,
which is where he tangled up with
Dingo, Bingo, Billy and Ben,
The Harmony Men!
Pete changed all that:
first chord he played, they knew;
first scream he screamed, they staggered back;
one waggle and it was all over;
and so was born
Pete and his Prodigal Men!

First it was small time:
bars, clubs and dives,
filled with disco cowboys
and disco dolls.
Pete's hair was jet black and greasy,
no face — just hair!
He dyed it pink when they played the Pink Casino.
The fans heard him on disc,
saw him on TV;
agents noted the adulation
and another idol was created.
Pete had made the Big Time.

Palladium,
Paris,
Las Vegas,
then back to the city Pete has sworn to flatten.
What a life!

Pills kept him going,
until he hit the bottle.
He sang off key;
he insulted the president of his fan club,
and sold the story to the Sunday papers;
rumours spread, dates got fewer,
so did Janes, Junes and Judies;
all they wanted was bread,
all Pete had were crusts.

'Give us more,' they cried,
and Pete was no meany,
so he borrowed off Dingo,
who borrowed off Bingo.
Billy and Ben joined the mailbag men
in a joint down rural Devon,
as guests of the Queen.
Pete was alone.

No boots with the cowboy tops cut off;
the brass studs fell off his leather jacket
one by one.
Finally . . .
no work, no money, no guitar,
no rent for the flat, no pills,
no Janes, Junes, or Judies,
no nothing — November.
The wind turned east.

After some hesitation Pete hitched a ride
back to Slitherslide Farm.

Was his old man mad?
No sir!
Pete was hugged and kissed,
and dad threw the biggest party ever.
New gear for Pete, even a new watch!

Meanwhile, big brother munched sour grapes;
boy, was he wild.
When he saw the fuss that his father was making
over his kid brother he flipped:
'The little slob comes crawling back,
absolutely skint, having wasted *our* money,
and what does dad do?
Celebrates!! That's all! 'Struth!'

So dad came out to see him
(sulking in the yard he was)
and dad said,
'Listen son, Pete's had it rough,
he's had to learn things the hard way,
he's mixed up;
Lend me a hand to sort him out. Okay?'

Pete came out and offered his brother a coke.
Pete grinned at his dad,
dad grinned at big brother,
but big brother wasn't sure what he ought to do . . .
not sure at all.

bABYLON

We have a
Hanging Garden!

I really must
get around to
fixing that window-box!

'WHERE NEITHER MOTH NOR RUST DOTH CORRUPT'

My religion's kept in mothballs,
Seldom sees the light of day;
But it won't rust, despite the dust,
Nor suffer from decay.
I took it out and dusted it
At Easter '83,
Then once again at Wembley when
I sang 'Abide with me'.

Appearances they average
Not even once-a-year,
But please don't call me 'pagan'
For I'm really quite sincere.
I'm certain when I'm old, or ill,
Or have a touch of gout,
I'll reach for my religion
And I'll throw the mothballs out.

I AM A COLOURED MAN

No matter what the racialists,
And other like-minded folk think,
Black is not classed as a colour,
But you can't say the same about pink.

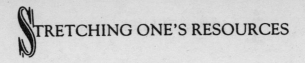STRETCHING ONE'S RESOURCES

We live in Birmingham
but we shop in Aberdeen!

It's the only way
we can think of
by which we can
make the housekeeping money
go a long way!

MY TELEPHONE

My telephone,
I am told,
links me with the world.

So does my humanity!

If only I employed
my humanity
as often as I use
my telephone.

Anarchy

The orchestra,
during the 1812 Overture,
fired their conductor!

Each section proceeded
to do its own thing:

The harpist plucked her eyebrows;
The strings bowed out;
The brass foundered;
The woodwinds blew their noses;
And the pianist,
Grand chap that he was,
read the score:
'Timpanists Five – Audience Nil.'

The full-time result?

DISCORD!

SOL

He, the source of life, offers direction,
Lord of day, and, sometimes, by reflection
serves the night; or gives the storm a rainbow;
He, the light, provides all health and growing,
sheds His warmth to thaw all coldness; throwing
shadows, glowing soft within his halo;
He, the fount of energy, emerging
fresh with dawn to set our spirits surging.

Enlightened we behold what He has done
and, opening wide our hearts, welcome the Son.

A selection of top titles from LION PUBLISHING

A TOUCH OF FLAME Jenny Robertson	£4.95	☐
GHETTO Jenny Robertson	£3.99	☐
C.S. LEWIS William Griffin	£5.95	☐
GEORGE MACDONALD William Raeper	£5.95	☐
CLEMO: A LOVE STORY Sally Magnusson	£3.95	☐
THE SHADOWED BED Jack Clemo	£3.95	☐
LILITH George MacDonald	£2.50	☐
PHANTASTES George MacDonald	£2.50	☐
SONS AND BROTHERS Elizabeth Gibson	£2.99	☐
TALIESIN Stephen Lawhead	£2.99	☐
MERLIN Stephen Lawhead	£3.50	☐
EMPYRION Stephen Lawhead	£4.99	☐
IN THE HALL OF THE DRAGON KING Stephen Lawhead	£2.99	☐
THE WARLORDS OF NIN Stephen Lawhead	£2.99	☐
THE SWORD AND THE FLAME Stephen Lawhead	£2.99	☐

All Lion paperbacks are available from your local bookshop or newsagent, or can be ordered direct from the address below. Just tick the titles you want and fill in the form.

Name (Block letters) _____

Address _____

_____

Write to Lion Publishing, Cash Sales Department, PO Box 11, Falmouth, Cornwall TR10 9EN, England.

Please enclose a cheque or postal order to the value of the cover price plus:

UK: 60p for the first book, 25p for the second book and 15p for each additional book ordered to a maximum charge of £1.90.

OVERSEAS: £1.25 for the first book, 75p for the second book plus 28p per copy for each additional book.

BFPO: 60p for the first book, 25p for the second book plus 15p per copy for the next seven books, thereafter 9p per book.

Lion Publishing reserves the right to show on covers and charge new retail prices which may differ from those previously advertised in the text or elsewhere, and to increase postal rates in accordance with the Post Office.